TELLING TREES

AN ILLUSTRATED GUIDE

Julius King

Illustrated by
Richard G. Sigafoos

Dover Publications, Inc.
Mineola, New York

Bibliographical Note

This Dover edition, first published in 2019, is an unabridged republication of the work originally published by William Sloane Associates, Inc., New York, in 1953.

Library of Congress Cataloging-in-Publication Data

Names: King, Julius, 1893–1964, author.
Title: Telling trees : an illustrated guide / Julius King, illustrated by Richard Sigafoos.
Description: Mineola, NY, Dover Publications, Inc., 2019. | This Dover edition, first published in 2019, is an unabridged republication of the work originally published by William Sloane Associates, Inc., New York, in 1953. | Summary: "A practical guide to identifying more than 100 American trees, this book presents clear, straightforward descriptions and hundreds of illustrations. Ideal for providing walkers and hikers with a quick, accurate reference"— Provided by publisher.
Identifiers: LCCN 2019019854 | ISBN 9780486838366
Subjects: LCSH: Trees—United States—Identification.
Classification: LCC QK115 .K483 2019 | DDC 582.16—dc23
LC record available at https://lccn.loc.gov/2019019854

Manufactured in the United States by LSC Communications
83836601
www.doverpublications.com

2 4 6 8 10 9 7 5 3 1

2019

BEFORE WE START FOR THE WOODS

This book is not for scientists, although they are welcome to use it if they like! It is rather for laymen who would like to go into the woods and get a definite answer to the question, "What tree is that?"

The language of this manual is not scientific, but common descriptive terms are used so that any reader may understand. This is not a handbook of listings of the commercial uses of the trees included in it; nor is it a poetic work about the grandeur, the stateliness and beauty of trees.

But since the woods are full of old friends that make our lives safer and more comfortable, since without trees our lives would be poor risks indeed, we have set out to make an identification book, pure, and we hope simple. Anyway, it is good to tell trees well enough to know an oak from a maple, a spruce from a pine, an ash from a sycamore. So picture and text are designed to help the reader say definitely "This is a *White* Pine," or "This is a *Black* Ash"; and everything that does not help identify a tree has been eliminated. Since most of us do our tree identifying in summer, the leaves are our best clues and they are the chief feature of our pictures. Take the book to the woods, or bring the leaves home and "put the finger" on them in an easy chair.

Somewhat over a hundred common American trees, including those of the West, are in the book. To assist in

3

determining sizes the artist has drawn a background scale of square inches. Count the squares and you have the size of leaf, needle, cone, flower, or fruit.

The main portion of the book deals with trees in summer in full leaf, but for those who wish to pursue the mystery of tree identification in the winter, my friend Rutherford Platt graciously permitted me to include his valuable key to trees in the snowy season. Mr. Platt is the author of the magnificent books *Our Flowering World* and *This Green World,* published by Dodd, Mead & Company. Our cordial gratitude is here expressed to Mr. Platt.

Our hope is that we will open a window on the woods to those who would enjoy a bit of intimate knowledge of trees, and need a simple book to help them.

The artist and I live and work in the country, among the hills of western New York and beside the waters of Chautauqua Lake—in the heart of what was once a virgin White Pine forest. Magnificient specimens of most northeastern trees are found within a hundred miles of us. These and other intimate arboreal acquaintances we now invite you to meet and learn to call by name.

JULIUS KING

Tall Timbers
Chautauqua, N. Y.
1953

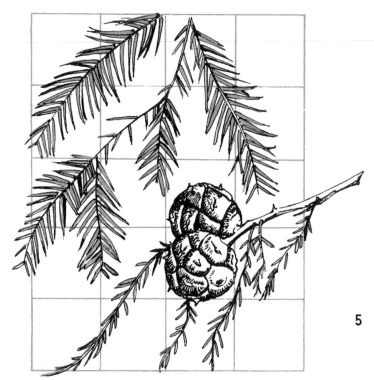

BALD CYPRESS • Taxodium distichum

You find Cypress in wet ground and swamps. The trunk is wide and rough at the base, tapering rapidly to its high slender column. Like the Tamarack it sheds its leaves every fall. Around the roots it produces steeple - shaped projections called "knees." Cones are almost round, the size of large

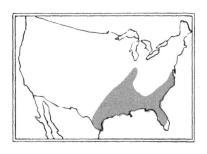

marbles. The needles are short (½ to ¾ inch), thin, light yellow-green, and grow in flat sprays. The branchlets on which needles grow are also shed in winter. Cypresses finally reach a height of 150 feet, with trunk diameter up to 10 feet.

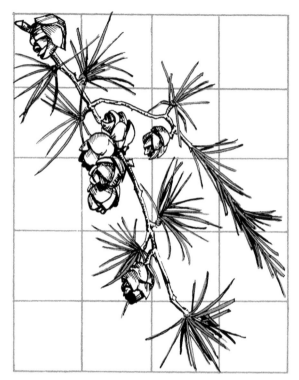

TAMARACK • Larix americana

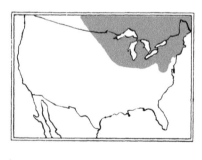

A Tamarack in summer has crisp, bright green needles (¾ to 1½ inches long) and is of graceful pyramidal shape up to 60 feet high. In the fall the needles turn a dull yellow and are shed, leaving the small ½-inch cones on the tree. Tamaracks like boggy swampy ground and thrive in marshes. In the North, however, they grow well in drained soil. Tamaracks and Cypresses are the only cone-bearing trees that shed their needles. Other names: LARCH; HACMATACK.

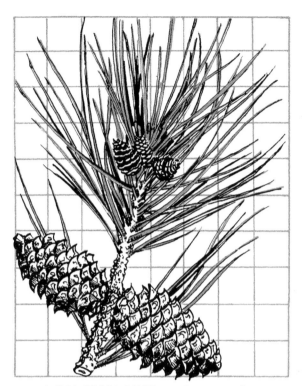

LOBLOLLY PINE • Pinus taeda

Pale green needles, 6 to 10 inches long, in clusters of *three,* slender, slightly twisted, stiff with sharp tips mark the Loblolly Pine. On cones which are 3 to 5 inches long, are stout recurved prickles. Loblolly Pines prefer low tidewater lands and swamps, but grow well in sandy soil too. The tall straight trunk reaches a height up to 100 feet, and a diameter up to 2 feet. Other names: OLD FIELD PINE; ROSEMARY PINE.

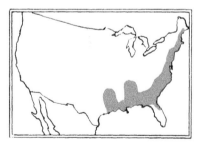

LODGEPOLE PINE • Pinus contorta

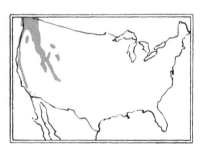

So-called because Indians used it for supports in tepees and lodges. This western tree is identified by its yellowish-green needles (2 inches long) which are *twisted* and come in twos. The cones are comparatively small (1 to 2 inches long) which cluster, and remain long on trees. Tall evergreen thickly branched from ground up, reaching an 80 foot height when mature.

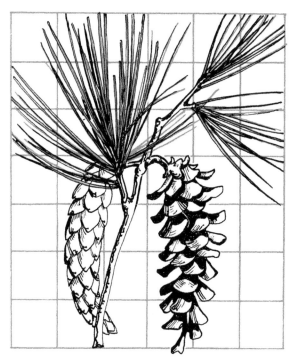

WHITE PINE • Pinus strobus

You tell the White Pine first by the cluster of *five needles,* soft, slender, bluish-green and 3 to 5 inches long. The cones are 4 to 6 inches in length, growing at *ends* of branches. Smoothest bark of all pines, dark gray on old trees, brownish-green on young. Reaches 125 feet in height with trunk

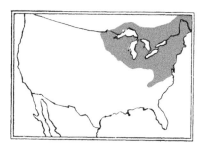

9

diameter sometimes as much as 4 feet. Grows best in sandy places, or disintegrated granite sand. A rapid grower, it is excellent for reforestation. Other name: WEYMOUTH PINE.

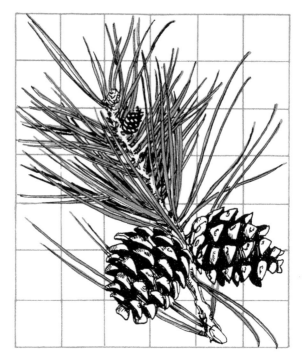

SHORTLEAF PINE • Pinus echinata

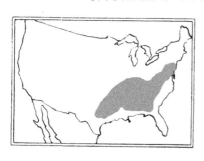

Dark blue - green needles in clusters of two (sometimes three) and 3 to 5 inches long, soft but with sharp tips. Very abundant small cones, 1½ to 2 inches long, with sharp prickles. Grows well in any soil, preferably sandy. Branches are slender at top of tall tapering trunk which reaches nearly 100 feet in height. Other names: YELLOW PINE; SPRUCE PINE.

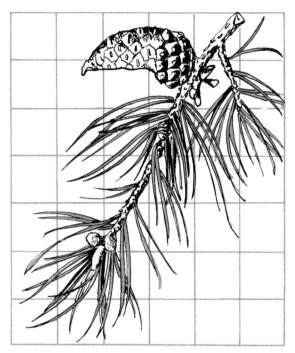

JACK PINE • Pinus banksiana

Dark *gray-green* needles (¾ to 1½ inches long) come in twos. In the mass the color is definitely *gray*. The cones are small (1½ to 2½ inches) and unfinished - looking. They too are *gray*. Jack Pines grow to 70 feet or so, but more often are stubby with many low branches. Earns its second name, Scrub Pine, in barren soil in eastern part of its range.

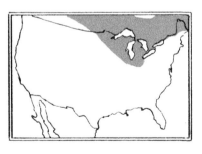

Other names: SCRUB PINE; GRAY PINE; NORTHERN SCRUB PINE.

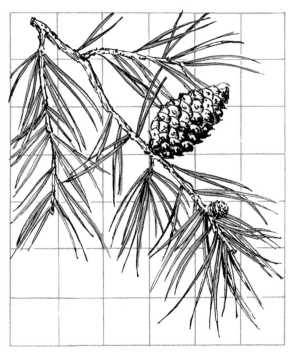

SCRUB PINE • Pinus virginiana

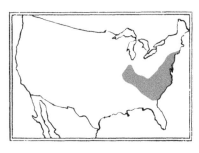

Spot the short (1½ to 3 inch) *twisted, bright green* needles, in pairs, on *purplish* branchlets. Then see the small (1 to 3 inch) cones, many of them *old*. Grows in sandy soil, even exhausted farmland, attaining a height of 35 feet or so. In Indiana, however, reaches twice that. Other name: JERSEY PINE.

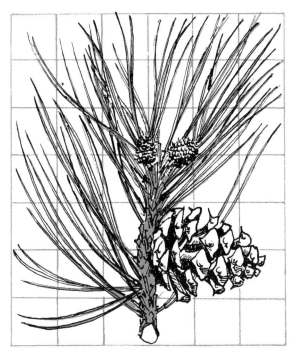

ROCK PINE • Pinus scopulorum

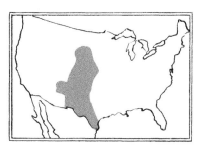

Very rough scaly plates of cinnamon - red mark the Rock Pine. So do the needles which come both in two's and three's (3 to 6 inches long), and quite *rigid* and stiff. The cones (2 to 4 inches) are somewhat ovoid in shape, and are covered with sharp prickles which curve *upward*. Generally about 60 feet high, rarely double that, and it grows on well-drained slopes. Other name: ROCKY MOUNTAIN YELLOW PINE.

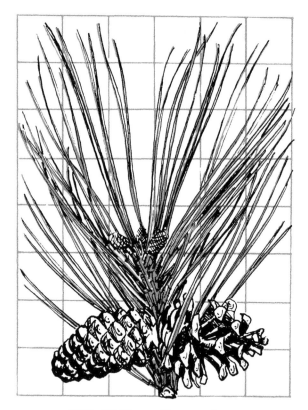

RED PINE • Pinus resinosa

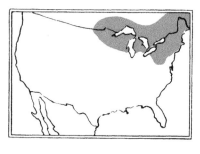

Prefers to grow in the open, not in forests, in dry, sandy, gravelly or rocky places—seldom on flat land. Needles (4 to 6 inches long) are *dark* green, shining, slender and flexible, and grow two to a bundle. The small cones (about 2 inches long) have no prickles. Bark is definitely *reddish*-brown, loaded with tannic acid. When cultivated grows rapidly. Other names: CANADIAN PINE; NORWAY PINE.

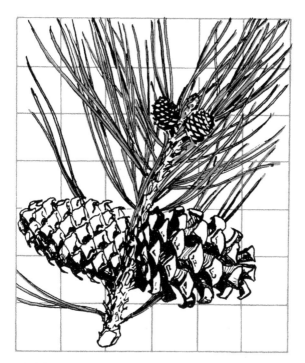

PONDEROSA PINE • Pinus ponderosa

A big one; frequently as tall as 200 feet straight up. Look for needles of dark green, anywhere from 5 to 10 inches long, and growing in bundles of three. The clustered cones are 3 to 5 inches long, erect until ripe, then turn downward. Twigs markedly rough to touch. Valuable clear lumber tree. Other name: WESTERN YELLOW PINE.

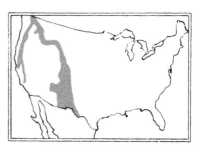

WESTERN LARCH • Larix occidentalis

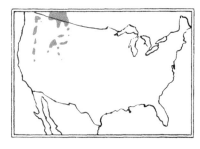

Biggest of the Larches or Tamaracks, reaching height of 200 feet on mastlike trunk. The needles are bright green (1 inch long), growing in groups or sprays. Needles are shed in autumn. Its cones are about 1½ inches long, with tiny leaf growing from under cone scales.

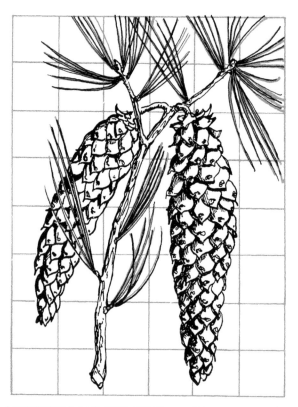

WESTERN WHITE PINE • Pinus monticola

Tall, straight, slender, this tree reaches for 100 or more feet of sky. Tree has a silvery look. The needles are slightly shorter (2 to 4 inches long) than the Eastern White Pine, but also come in bundles of *five*. These are bluish-green with silvery appearance at a distance. The cones (6 to 10 inches long)

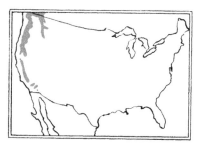

are twice the size of the eastern variety; they also hang downward on short stems. Other names: SILVER PINE; FINGER-CONE PINE.

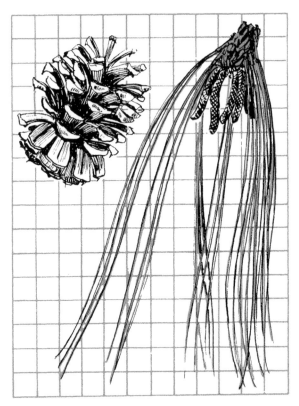

YELLOW PINE • Pinus palustris

18

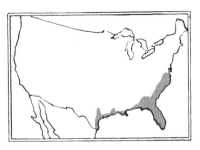

Slender needles often 15 inches long come in drooping clusters of *three,* vivid green in color. These tall, straight, rapid-growing southern trees bear large cones, 6 to 10 inches long, each scale with a sharp pointed *upward-curving* prickle. Important source of lumber, turpentine, rosin and (lately) paper.

Other names: LONGSTRAW PINE; LONGLEAF PINE.

WHITE SPRUCE • Picea canadensis

All Spruces differ from Pines in having needles placed *singly,* and they grow thickly on *all sides* of branches. White Spruce is beautiful but foliage has unpleasant smell. Needles, dark green (⅓ to ¾ inch long), placed *spirally* on stems, somewhat thicker on top side as lower needles twist upward.

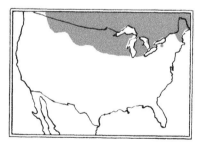

Cones are 2-inch *cylinders.* This tree attains 150 foot height and diameter of 3 feet. Other name: Skunk Spruce.

BLUE SPRUCE • Picea pungens

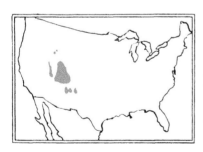

Perfect pyramid in shape, new growth at branch tips, silvery blue-green. Needles are four-sided and rigid (½ to 1 inch long) curved and spiny. Cones, large for spruces, are 2 to 4 inches long. Grows to 100 foot height, rarely 150. Outside its range it is planted ornamentally in parks and lawns. Other name: SILVER SPRUCE.

DOUGLAS FIR • Pseudotsuga taxifolia

A truly big one — a straight trunk up to 250 feet tall. Branches close to ground in open, high up in forests. Gray-green needles, underside of which are like those of Hemlock; these grow in *spirals* on twigs. Cones are 2 to 4 inches long, and hang downward. The cone scales have triple-pronged leaves growing out of them.

RED SPRUCE • Picea rubens

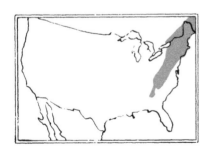

A Spruce that attains a height of 75 feet at the southern end of its range, and is little more than a scrub in far North. Needles are *four-sided* (1½ to ⅝ inches long) standing out from *all sides* of branch *pointing forward*. Reddish-brown bark, red twigs, pale red wood. Cones smaller than White Spruce (1¼ to 2 inches long) and more oblong. Red Spruce cones fall the first winter.

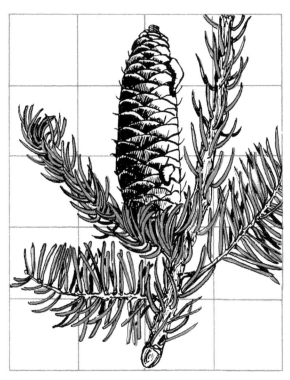

BALSAM FIR • Abies balsamea

Bark on mature trees is reddish-brown with frequent "blisters" holding clear crystal resin. Cones oblong cylindrical, dark *purple* (2 to 4 inches long), thickly carried on *upper side* of branches. Needles are flat, shiny green above, silvery below, and very fragrant even when dried, arranged *spirally*

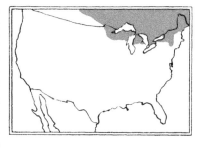

around branches. Grows to 50 or 60 feet and is short-lived. Other name: BALSAM.

RED CEDAR • Juniperus virginiana

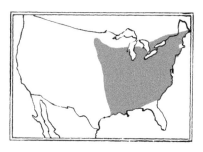

Here's where cedar chests come from! Red Cedar carries *two kinds* of leaves—growing opposite—thick scaly ones, and also sharp awl-like needles. The latter are rigid and long pointed (¼ to ¾ inch); the scale-shaped are very small and crowded on branchlet. Has a dark blue berry about ¼ inch in diameter with sweet resinous taste. Varies from shrub size to 100 foot tree. Bark is light reddish-brown, somewhat scaly.

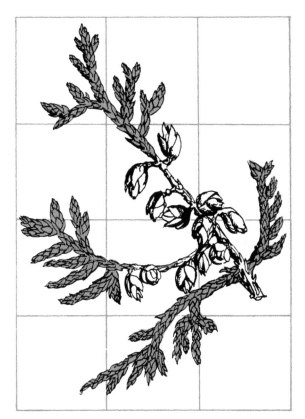

NORTHERN WHITE CEDAR • Thuja occidentalis

Leaves grown on *fanlike* branchlets, and are thick and scaly and very close together. Bright yellow-green most of year; early spring, brownish. Crushed leaves are very fragrant. Cones are small, less than ½ inch long. Each "fan" of branchlets or plane is erect, some are vertical, and there

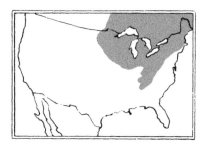

are no "air holes" visible through the tree which attains height of 50 to 60 feet. Other name: ARBORVITAE.

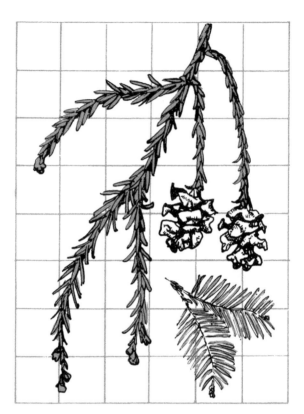

SEQUOIA • Sequoia sempervirens

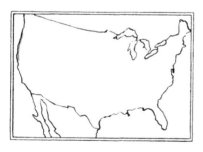

America's biggest tree grows to
a height of 350 feet with trunks
20 feet in diameter. Needs sea
fog for healthy growth; hence
its West Coast habitat. Tree is
rigid and not moved by ordi-
nary wind. Needles of two
kinds—some ½ to 1 inch long
like Hemlock needles in flat
sprays; some scalelike, similar
to Arborvitaes. Cones are small (1 inch long) and grow on ends
of twigs. Other name: REDWOOD. Note: BIG TREES (*Sequoia
gigantea*) are found only in Sequoia National Park.

JUNIPER • Juniperus communis

Leaves (½ to ¾ inch long) are sharp, awl-like and arranged *around* twig in threes. Juniper is sometimes a 25 foot high tree, or more often a low wide-spreading shrub. Carries dark blue berries (¼ inch in diameter), resinous, aromatic and sweet-tasting. Widely distributed in northern half of entire world. Other name: GROUND CEDAR.

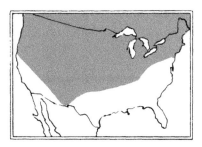

AMERICAN HOLLY • Ilex opaca

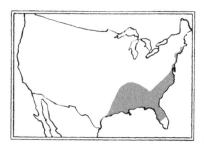

Anyone who knows Christmas greenery knows Holly. Before developing the characteristic red berries, Holly bears small greenish-white flowers in May or June. The red fruit-berry grows *singly* on short stalks on the twigs. The leaves with spiny points and smooth shiny surfaces of dark green are evergreen. Sometimes 50 feet tall, but a slow grower.

HEMLOCK • Tsuga canadensis

Resident of swamps, gorges and rocky woods, with dark reddish and roughly ridged bark, Hemlock carries *flat* sprays of short needles (dark green above, and paler beneath). Under side of each needle has *two* parallel light stripes. The many small (¾ inch) cones all *hang* downward. Hemlocks reach 100 foot height.

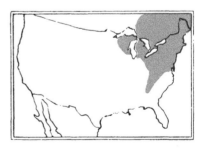

BLACK WALNUT • Juglans nigra

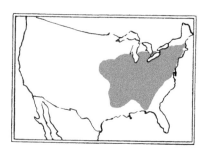

Compound leaves, 1 to 2 feet long, each composed of seventeen (more or less) leaflets (2 to 4 inches long). Leaflets are slightly toothed, and are aromatic when bruised. Trunk, attaining 150 foot height, is dark brown with prominent ridges. Characteristic nut-case is light yellow-green and almost round; the nut is round-oval and deeply carved—and delicious.

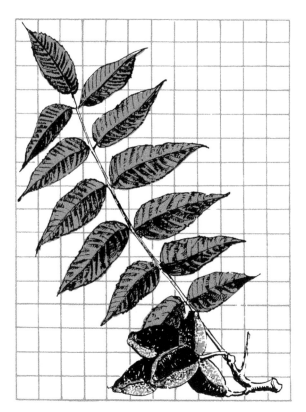

BUTTERNUT • Juglans cinerea

Compound leaves somewhat shorter (11 to 17 inches) than Walnut, with eleven to nineteen yellowish-green leaflets (2 to 4 inches long) which are slightly *sticky* at first. Twigs are yellow-brown, smooth, shiny, and have small round white spots. Long catkins are pollen-bearing. Heavily sculptured nuts come in sticky husks, and grow in clusters. Other names: WHITE WALNUT; OIL NUT.

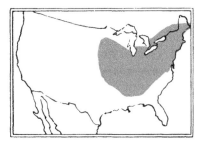

BITTERNUT HICKORY • Hicoria cordiformis

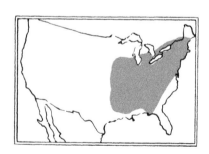

Compound leaves, 6 to 10 inches long, with seven to eleven *lance-shaped* dark green leaflets (2 to 6 inches long) noticeably saw-toothed. Nuts almost round with very bitter meats, come in smooth round reddish-brown husks. Grows to 100 feet, 2 or 3 feet in diameter, with brownish-gray bark marked by close diamond-shaped ridges. Grows in any soil and is very hardy.

SHAGBARK HICKORY • Hicoria ovata

Easy to identify by the big platelike strips of bark which have *attached* firm *upper* ends. Grows tall, 100 feet and 2 to 3 feet in diameter, on low hillsides and along banks of streams. Compound leaves, usually with five leaflets, the outer three being broadest. Husk of nut nearly round and splits in four parts. Nuts are delicious.

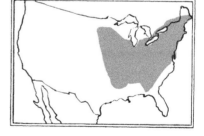

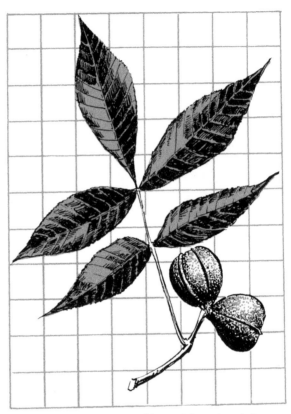

PIGNUT HICKORY • Hicoria glabra

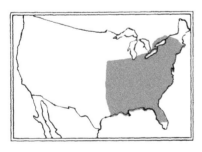

An upland tree with compound leaves 8 to 12 inches long, and five to seven leaflets, sharp-toothed and rather lance-shaped. Leaves are *hairy* but stem is smooth. Husks are oblong and do not split to the base to drop out the brownish thick-shelled nuts. Some taste bitter, others pleasantly edible. A tall tree, growing to 100 foot height—in open it forks quite near the ground. Bark is dark gray and smoother than other Hickories.

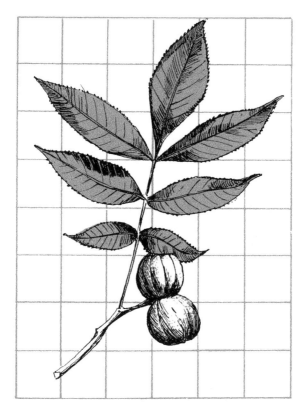

PALE-LEAF HICKORY • Hicoria villosa

A forest tree usually, no taller than 50 feet at maturity. Bark is gray-brown, quite rough and with scaly ridges. Compound leaves 6 to 10 inches long with slightly hairy leaflets, ordinarily seven, usually lance-shaped and saw-edged. Almost round husks with thin skin that splits nearly to base, releasing sweet, edible nuts with thick shells.

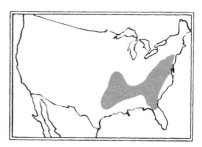

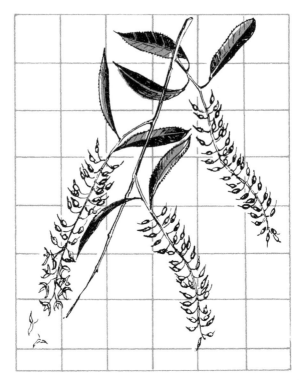

ALMOND-LEAF WILLOW • Salix amygdaloides

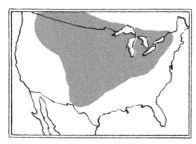

Along streams and shores, in close company with the Black Willow, note first the peach-leaf shape of these leaves (2 to 6 inches long), shiny light green above, pale beneath. Leaf edges are fine-toothed. Bark is ridged but lighter in color and smoother than the Black Willow. Main use of wood is for charcoal.

SANDBAR WILLOW • Salix longifolia

More often a shrub than a tree, this willow with smooth bark occasionally grows to 50 foot height. The leaves, long and slender, taper at *both ends,* and are mostly smooth. Usually the first to spring up on sandbars, building up soil until Cottonwoods take hold. Wood is good only for fuel and charcoal. Other name: LONG-LEAF WILLOW.

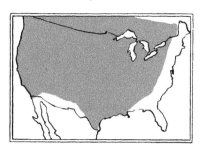

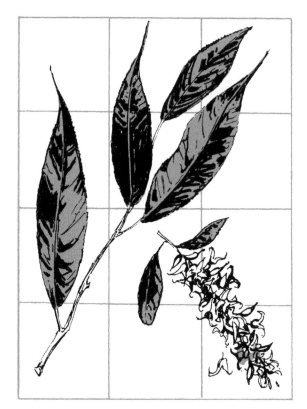

SHINING WILLOW • Salix lucida

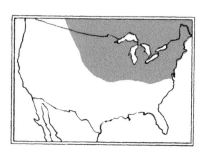

A word about willows—there are so many and they are so similar that no quick identification is possible on some of the varieties. The Shining Willow, however, has dark green, leathery shiny leaves, with the midrib beneath very prominent. Tree is bushy, with smooth bark, about 20 feet high at most. Other names: GLOSSY-LEAF WILLOW; GLOSSY WILLOW.

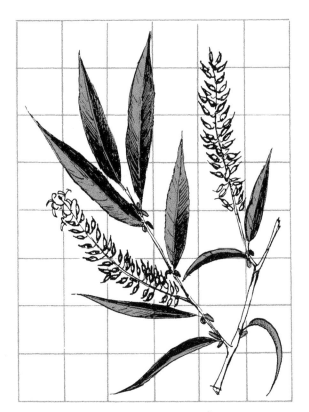

BLACK WILLOW • Salix nigra

Our biggest streamside willow, sometimes over 100 feet high, more often many-trunked from huge low base. Foliage is light green and drooping, the leaves (3 to 6 inches long), thin, lance-shaped, occasionally curved like sickles. At base, or stem joint on the twig, there is pair of *tiny leaflike* parts.

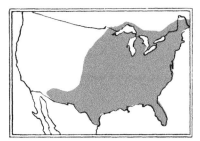

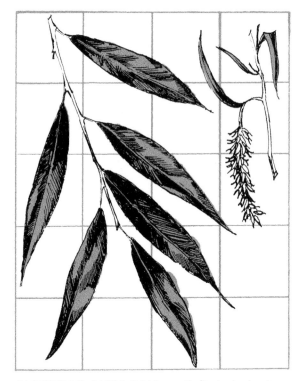

WEEPING WILLOW • Salix babylonica

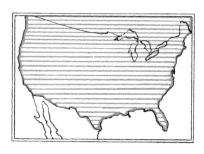

An easily identified species, with thick trunk, quickly dividing, and the branchlets droop and hang down. The long leaves, twigs and blossoms are all delicate and slender, and the whole tree seems to be in motion even in a light breeze. Its feathery green shows encouragingly early in the spring.

Other names: BABYLON WILLOW; NAPOLEON'S WILLOW; RING WILLOW.

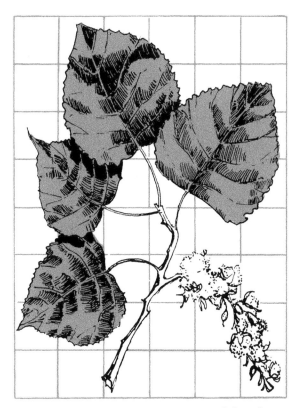

COTTONWOOD • **Populus deltoides**

Found in rich moist bottom land and stream banks, the Cottonwood lifts itself to 100 feet with thick 6 to 8 foot trunks. The *broad* leaves have *roundish* teeth that point *forward*. Base of leaf rather square, not heart shaped. Both sides of leaf shiny green and smooth. Name comes from the

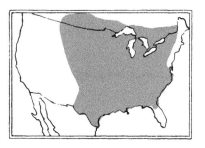

mass of brown seeds which release a cotton-like down. Other names: Carolina Poplar; Necklace Poplar.

LOMBARDY POPLAR • Populus nigra

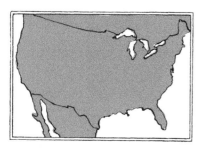

All branches of the Lombardy Poplar grow straight up, giving it a characteristic shape recognizable at any distance. The leaf is very broad in relation to its length; base is wedge shape, and tip is pointed. Often reaches 100 foot height with thick buttressed trunks (6 or 8 feet in diameter). In America it has *no seeds,* but is grown exclusively from slips and cuttings.

BALSAM POPLAR • Populus balsamifera

Another riverside tree by preference, the Balsam Poplar in southern part of range is a 50 footer, in the North and West 100. Leaves 3 to 5 inches long, 1½ to 3 inches wide, deep dark green, *thicker* at margins, *rounded* at base. Produces masses of snowy "cotton." Tree and leaves have balsamy smell. Other names: BALSAM; TACMAHAC.

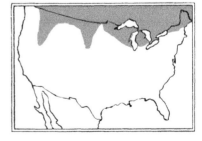

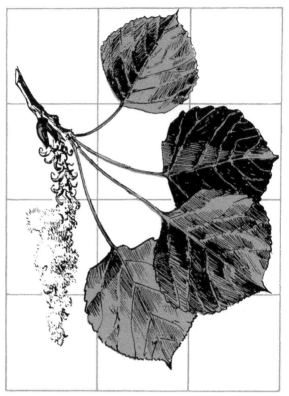

QUAKING ASP • Populus tremuloides

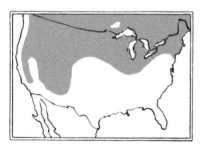

Long slender leaf stems or petioles which are flattened allow the bright green leaves to flutter in the lightest breeze. "It trembles like an aspen." Leaves are roundish, with sharp-toothed margins and abrupt points. Bark is dark and rough near ground; above, pale greenish-brown, almost white. Thick stands of aspens grow over burned ground, and at edges of woods.

45

ASPEN • Populus grandidentata

Teeth on the leaf margins larger, deeper than on Quaking Asp. Long petioles slightly compressed permit leaves to tremble also. Many grow together in thickets, seeded from the long pendant feathery stems that blow away in the wind. Bark is grayish-green and smooth above, fissured and

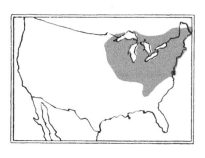

dark near the ground. Other name: LARGE-TOOTHED POPLAR.

HOP HORNBEAM • Ostrya virginiana

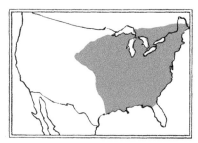

Note the forward-facing teeth of leaves, with veins arranged like feathers. Has pale fruit like hops containing tiny brown nuts. The bark is rough, formed of narrow, loose, long scales. Grows in well drained places, and sometimes reaches 60 to 70 feet in height. Check the hardness of the wood with your knife. Other name: IRONWOOD.

WHITE BIRCH • Betula populifolia

Leaves have flattish bases, spreading teeth, and are triangular in shape. Long stems or petioles allow wind to agitate the leaves. Bark is whitish-gray, with dark marks under branches. You may peel off bark in layers in smooth sections of the trunk, but near ground trunk is rough and 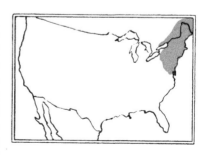 fissured. Other names: OLD FIELD BIRCH; GRAY BIRCH.

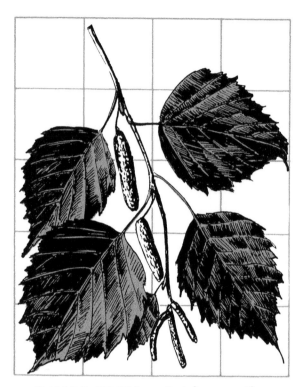

CANOE BIRCH • Betula papyrifera

48

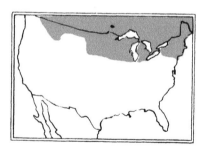

Bark is a creamy, rather chalky white with yellowish tint, and peels off easily in many layers. There are many horizontally raised tiny ridges. Mature tree is usually 50 to 60 feet high, rarely up to 100. The fruit-spikes look conelike, and the leaves with toothy edges are triangular. Other names: PAPER BIRCH; WHITE BIRCH.

49

YELLOW BIRCH • Betula lutea

Ribbon-like strips and curls on main trunk are characteristic of the Yellow Birch, though the branches and twigs are smooth. Leaves are somewhat oval, cut in or heart-shape at base. Grows to about the 100 foot mark. Fruit is an erect, short-stalked spike (called a strodile). Prefers rich moist

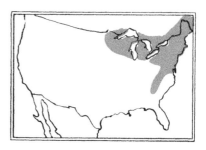

uplands for best growth. Other names: GRAY BIRCH; SILVER BIRCH.

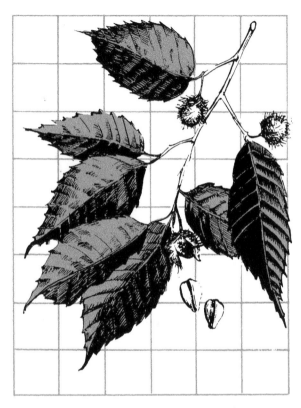

BEECH • Fagus grandifolia

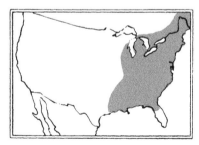

Learn the look of the smooth, silvery gray of the bark and you can always tell a Beech. The leaves are as pictured, and veined like feathers. Turn yellow in fall, and sometimes hang on tree all winter. Nut is triangular, less than an inch long, enclosed in hairy husk. Young trees do not fruit.

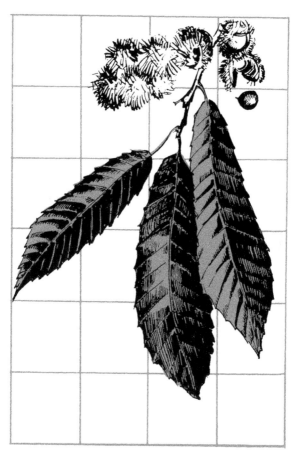

51

CHINQUAPIN • Castanea pumila

Usually a spreading shrub instead of a tree. Long narrow leaves with slender pointed teeth. Spiky clusters with sharp spines which contain a single dark brown roundish nut, slightly hairy at tip. Nut, while small, is very pleasant to taste. In some sections develops into a tree up to 40 feet in height, but this is not common.

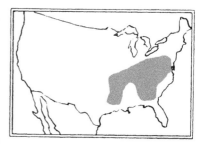

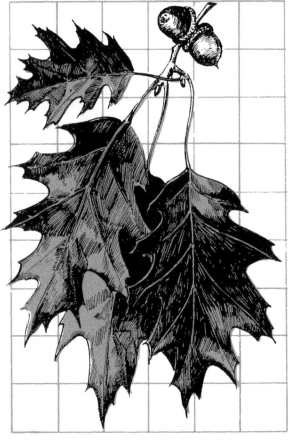

RED OAK • Quercus rubra

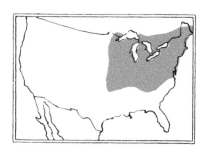

Grows best on well-drained banks of rivers and streams. Acorn is very large, and in shallow cup. The kernel is white and so bitter that even squirrels won't eat it! Two types of leaves—one narrow, one broad—but all usually have three teeth at points. In fall, turn rich purplish-red. Grows to 100 foot height and when growing alone has large, wide-spreading branches. A rapid grower.

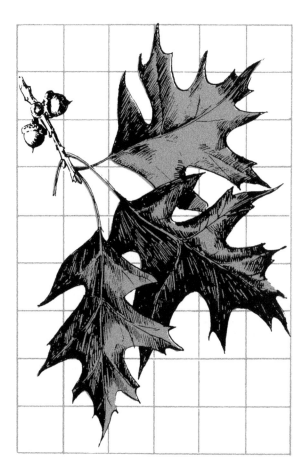

PIN OAK • Quercus palustris

Note the broad acorns in wide shallow cups shaped like saucers. The leaves are borne on rather long stems, and have five to nine lobes with bristle points separated by wide, deep clefts. Bark is comparatively smooth, on trees that attain 60 or 70 feet of height. The twigs of the bare tree in winter, ac-

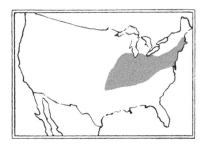

cording to one authority, look like pins in a pincushion—hence the name. Other names: SWAMP OAK; SWAMP SPANISH OAK; WATER OAK.

SCARLET OAK • Quercus coccinea

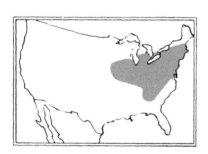

The acorn is *half-enclosed* by the large cup, sometimes is *striped* and frequently grows in pairs. Leaves quite similar to Pin Oak, but are deeply cut, the rounded depressions reaching nearly to the middle rib. 70 to 80 feet in height. In fall the tree lives up to its name, turning scarlet and staying red for a long period.

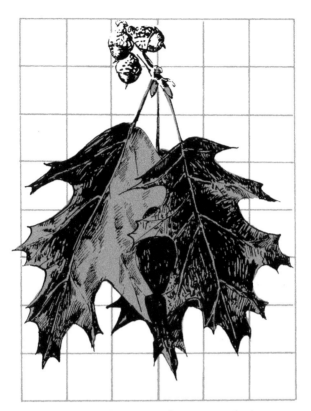

YELLOW OAK • Quercus velutina

Acorns (½ to ¾ inch long) are *half-covered* by the rather *rough* cups. Some leaves as much as 10 inches long, but closely resembling those of Scarlet Oak. Grows to 70 to 100 foot height, bark is ridged and dark brown to blackish. In fall the large, shiny, dark green leaves turn red, some orange and brown. Other name: BLACK OAK.

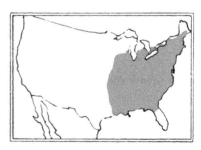

56

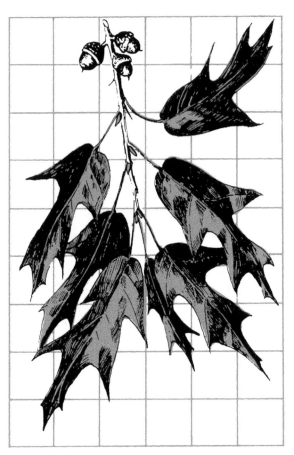

SPANISH OAK • Quercus falcata

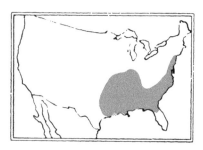

Acorns (½ inch long) are about *one-third* enclosed by the thin cup. Leaves are of many shapes on same branch, shiny dark green above and grayish beneath. Looking at tree as a whole, note the *drooping* appearance of the leaves as on no other Oak.

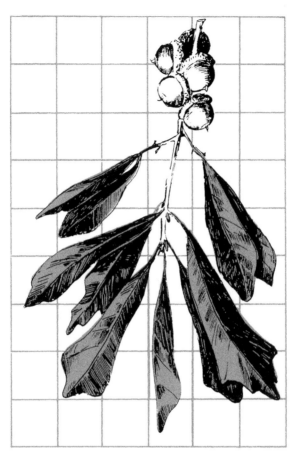

WATER OAK • Quercus nigra

Many of its acorns are half-globes (hemispheric) not quite half-enclosed by the flat saucer-shaped cup. The leaves are of many forms and sizes. Mature leaves smooth and dark green above, clinging long to the tree. A bottom-land resident attaining about 75 foot height. Other names: DUCK OAK; POSSUM OAK.

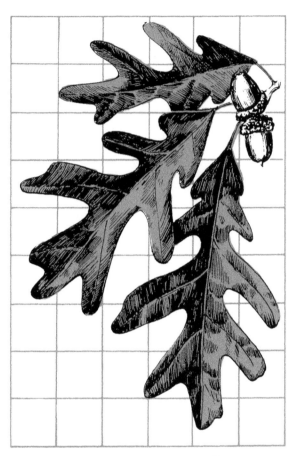

WHITE OAK • Quercus alba

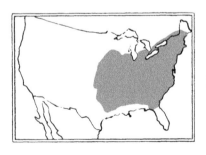

Acorns (¾ inch long) are elongated oval in form, in flat *warty* cups that cover about one-quarter of acorn. Leaves have pronounced rounded lobes, with the depression-cuts at an oblique angle. Many are as long as 9 inches, smooth dark green, turning rich dark red in fall. Reaches for more than 100 feet of sky, and is best of the Oaks for commercial use.

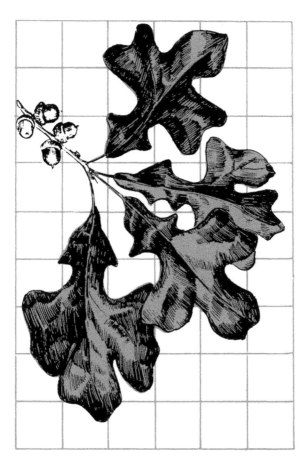

POST OAK • Quercus stellata

Upper three lobes of leaves look like big clover or fleur de lis, of shining dark green above, the underside yellowish-gray, often with tiny hairs. Acorn cups usually have no stems but are attached by the base, and the nut itself is half-enclosed in the half-sphere (hemispheric) cup. Bark is *checked* in squares. Grows to 100 foot height.

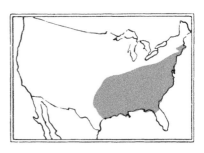

BUR OAK • Quercus macrocarpa

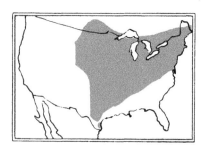

60

Large acorns, almost entirely enveloped in cups with *rough mossy* fringes, tell this tree instantly. The leaves too are unique. Near the stem (or petiole) the leaf is deeply carved—almost to the mid-rib—while at upper end leaf is much broader. A tree reaching over 125 feet around Indiana, in general is much smaller. In East prefers rich bottom lands for its best growth. Other names: MOSSY CUP OAK; OVER-CUP OAK.

CHESTNUT OAK • Quercus prinus

Acorns rather large, more oblong than round, and about
one-third enveloped by the
deep cup which is rough and
scaly. The leaves have wavy
edges, not cut in, and closely
resemble Chestnut leaf. Usually 60 to 70 feet in height with
rough prominently ridged bark,
and grows best on well-drained
uplands. Other name: ROCK OAK.

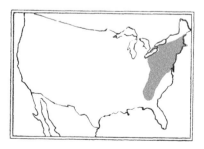

SWAMP WHITE OAK • Quercus bicolar

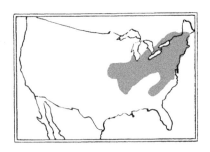

Leaf gives broad effect, with a wavy edge, not deeply cut-in like the White Oak. Acorns are large and are held in a deep cup that encloses half the nut. Upper side of leaves is shining dark yellow-green, underside lighter and slightly hairy. Medium height (50 to 70 feet) and grows best with "wet feet."

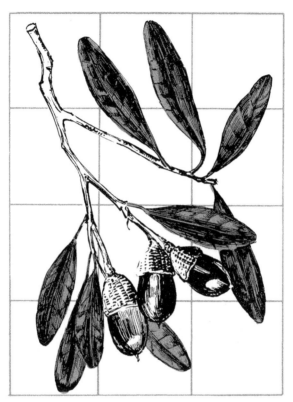

LIVE OAK • Quercus virginiana

Look for tremendous *spread*, not height. Big branches, trunks in themselves, start near base of massive trunk and reach out horizontally. Leaves more like Willow than Oak, usually with smooth edges. Acorns are small, light brown, about one-third covered by the cup, each of which has a pronounced stem.

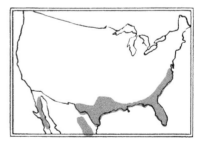

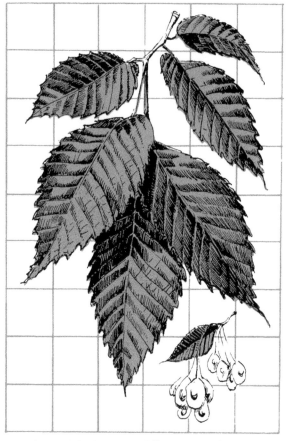

WHITE ELM • Ulmus americana

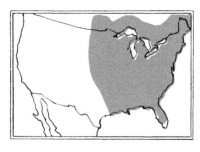

Start with shape of this tree—like a symmetrical vase. Branches droop gracefully. Leaves are evenly saw-toothed, but typically are slightly lopsided. Grows tall—up to 125 feet—often in small groves, and thrives with wet roots. This is one of the favorite American trees. Other names: GRAY ELM; WATER ELM; AMERICAN ELM; SWAMP ELM.

SLIPPERY ELM • Ulmus fulva

Leaves, rough to the touch, are regular and symmetrical in shape, and not so sharply toothed as White Elm. Cut a piece of bark—it will be fragrant and the inner bark will be moist like mucilage, and is often chewed. Grows to 60 or 70 feet, and is somewhat similar in shape to White Elm, but not so graceful in appearance. Other name: RED ELM.

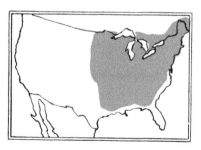

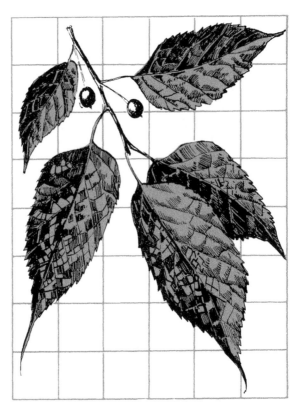

HACKBERRY • *Celtis occidentalis*

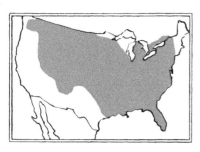

Variegated, spotted leaves with sharp-toothed edges, slightly lopsided, suggest the Elm, to which family it belongs. More definite identification is of the long-stemmed purple berry with yellowish meat, pleasant to the taste. Tree has very rough bark, and although occasionally 100 feet tall, is usually just of average height. Other names: SUGARBERRY; NETTLE TREE; HOOP ASH.

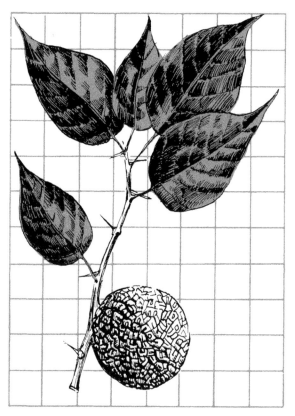

OSAGE ORANGE • Toxylon pomiferum

The scaly bark, deeply ridged, orange-brown in color, is rich in tannin; the leaves are poplar-shaped, toothless, but with short thorns at the base of the stem. The "male" tree carries seed-bearing flowers, the "female" small round fuzzy seeds. These latter grow into a hard round "orange," light green in color, 3 to 5 inches in diameter. Other names: BOW-WOOD; HEDGE TREE; OSAGE APPLE.

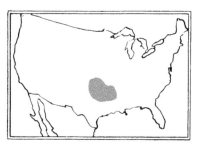

CUCUMBER TREE • Magnolia acuminata

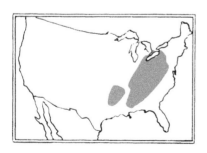

Large shiny green leaves in abundant number, give tree a dense effect. In late spring has tulip-shaped flowers later developing into greenish - red elongated fruit, which splits to free the large berries that hang by slender threads. The black inner seeds are distributed by birds. Grows tall—up to 75 feet—with straight column of trunk. Other name. MOUNTAIN MAGNOLIA.

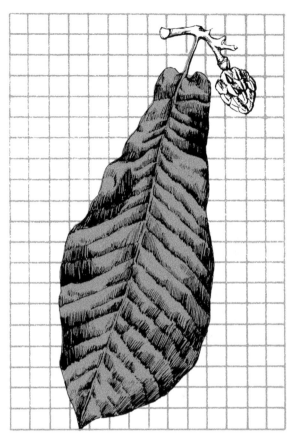

MAGNOLIA • Magnolia macrophylla

Huge leaves—up to 20 inches long — bright smooth green above, much lighter and slightly hairy beneath. Flowers are dinner-plate size, bell-shaped and waxy white. Bark is comparatively smooth and close-textured. Flowers are followed by pinkish almost round fruit, which opens and exposes bright red seeds hanging by thin threads. Not tall—30 to 50 feet—and grows natively in rich soil. Other name: LARGE-LEAF MAGNOLIA.

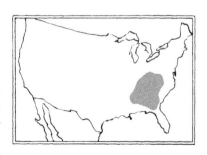

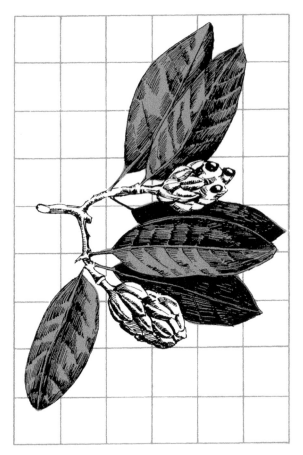

70

SWEET BAY • Magnolia virginiana

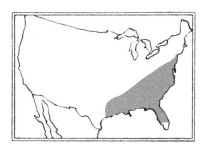

Smooth 3 to 6 inch leaves, oblong-oval in shape, not toothed on edges. Shiny dark green above, whitish and slightly hairy beneath. Flowers are offwhite, slightly creamy in color and about 2 inches across. Fruit is smooth, reddish, cone-shaped which opens to scatter its enclosed seeds. Crushed leaves are fragrant—like bay rum. Other name: SWAMP MAGNOLIA.

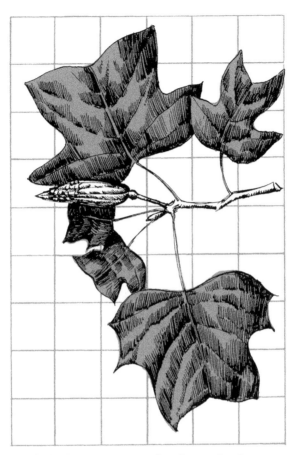

TULIP TREE • Liriodendron tulipifera

Leaves are mostly squarish, though some are gracefully notched with rounded cuts. The flower is tulip-shaped, about 2 inches deep, and the fruit is an elongated cone standing erect. The tulip attains great and massive growth, reaching as much as 175 feet, with big branches 75 feet from the ground. Other names: WHITE WOOD; TULIP POPLAR.

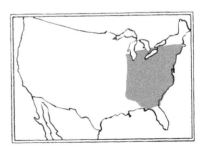

PAPAW • Asimina triloba

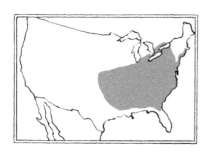

Leaves are large, lance-shaped, and 8 to 12 inches long, smooth light green in color. The fruit is shaped somewhat like a short small cucumber, with yellow meat within, in which the flat, wavy, 1-inch seeds are held. The odor is pungent. Papaw is usually a large shrub, growing in shade of other taller trees. Related to the Papaya.

SWAMP BAY • Persea pubescens

Leaves pointed at both ends, 5 to 10 inches long, shiny dark green above, pale and hairy underneath. Rather rusty along the main veins. Fruit is a dark blue berry on long stem, with aromatic flesh. Never tall, but thickly leaved and with straight branches. Sometimes 30 to 40 feet tall, growing in swamps and marshes.

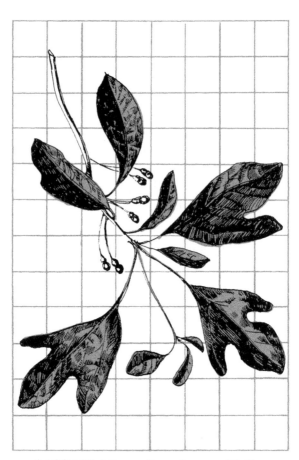

SASSAFRAS • Sassafras variifolium

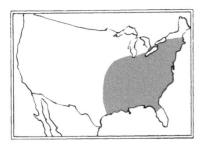

Root and bark have aromatic taste and odor. Leaves are of three shapes — oval, mitten-form with *one* large "thumb," and other leaves with two "thumbs." You may find all three on the same twig. Fruit is a pendant, dark blue berry suspended on rather long stem. Average height of mature trees about 50 feet.

WITCH HAZEL • Hamamelis virginiana

Leaves have short stems (petioles) and wavy edges. Smooth dark green above, and hairy on veins on under side. The golden colored *stringy* flowers develop late in summer or early fall. The seed capsules are dull brown, out of which the seeds *pop* explosively, like shooting wet orange seeds by pinching with fingers. Usually a large shrub, only occasionally a 25 foot tree.

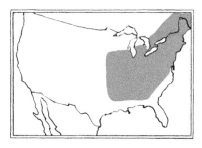

SWEET GUM • Liquidambar styraciflua

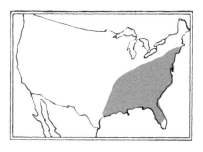

Leaves like Maple's but much longer points—shape really reminds most of starfish. The pollen-bearing flowers are on catkins, the seed-bearing in round heads on long stems. These heads develop into round fruits a little over an inch in diameter. A tall tree, often over 100 feet high, growing in rich moist soil. Leaves turn bright red and yellow in fall. Other names: BILSTED; LIQUIDAMBAR; RED GUM.

SYCAMORE • Platanus occidentalis

The bark is your best clue to the Sycamore. Great smooth white patches stand out, with irregular plates of brown bark here and there. The seed blossoms develop into round long-stemmed buttony balls, holding the seeds for winter scattering. Sycamores are stately and grow to well over

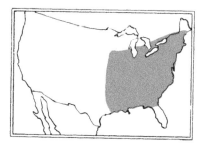

100 feet in height. Other names: Buttonwood; Button Ball Tree; American Plane Tree.

FRAGRANT CRAB • Pyrus coronaria

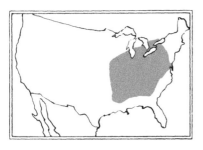

Leaves (3 to 4 inches long) resemble grape leaves, with teeth of varied cuts, and generally fitting into a drawn triangle, the base being somewhat rounded. Twigs have spiny points. Fruit is pale green, with sweet smelling skin but bitter taste, and is waxy to the touch. White or pinkish blossoms in late spring. Height up to 25 or 30 feet. Other names: WILD CRAB APPLE; AMERICAN CRAB.

PRAIRIE CRAB • Pyrus ioensis

Leaves oval-oblong, teeth not
so pronounced as Fragrant
Crab's; much more rounded at
base. Very fragrant blossoms.
The apples are yellowish-
green, with waxy surface and
fragrant smell—but the taste
is bitter and unpleasant. Grows
20 to 30 feet in height. Numerous thorns throughout the
twisted branches.

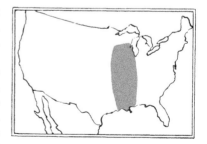

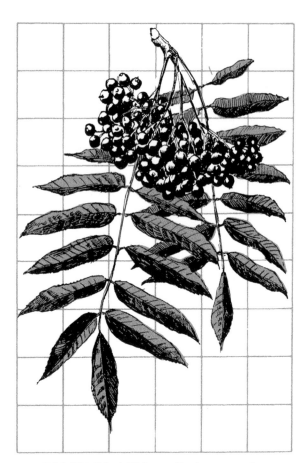

MOUNTAIN ASH • Sorbus americana

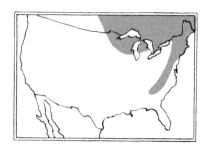

This tree has compound leaves (6 to 10 inches long) with narrow leaflets like Willow leaves. Flowers grow in thick clusters in May, and the fruit, a bright orange-red, which develops from these clusters, matures in fall and sometimes remains in winter. Grows on slopes and even swamps in North, and reaches a height of about 25 feet. Other name: AMERICAN MOUNTAIN ASH.

81

SERVICE-BERRY • Amelanchier canadensis

In spring stands out as a mass of small white flowers. Other name, Shad-bush, indicates its season of bloom—when the shad spawns! Fruit is a small (¼ inch) berry of dark purple color with smooth skin—a favorite of the birds. Usually a small tree, and likes well drained locations to grow best.

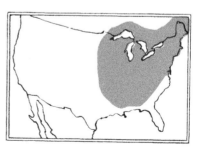

Other names: SHAD-BUSH; SHAD BLOW; JUNEBERRY.

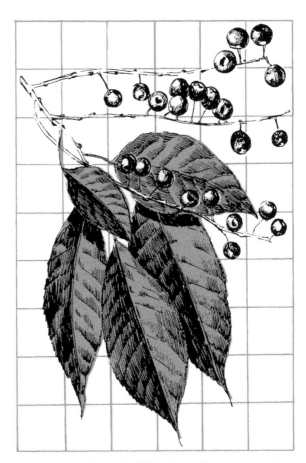

WILD BLACK CHERRY • Prunus serotina

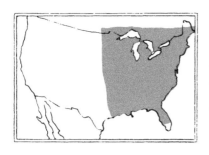

This one grows big, sometimes 90 to 100 feet tall, with scaly-barked trunk. Leaves are 2 to 5 inches long, oval to lance-shaped, with toothed edges, shiny dark green above, paler beneath, and the stems showing small reddish bulges. Small white flowers in clusters around the stem. Fruit is small (⅓ to ½ inch), reddish-black, purple meat, pungent taste.

WILD RED CHERRY • Prunus pennsylvanica

This one grows small (30 to 40 feet) and bark is typically cherry, of rich wine color, with horizontally raised ridges, peels off like Birch bark. Grows in well-drained places and at edge of woods. Leaves, round at base, are lance-shaped, have tiny unequal teeth. Small white flowers.

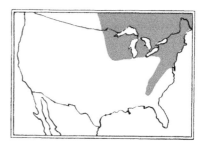

Fruit is a light red, almost transparent, and very sharp to taste. Other names: PIN CHERRY; BIRD CHERRY; PIGEON CHERRY.

CHOKE CHERRY • *Prunus virginiana*

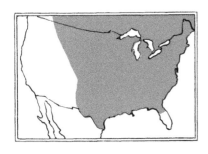

This is a small one, usually a large shrub, trunk usually leaning or crooked. When it rarely becomes a tree, the bark is mottled dark gray with lighter spots. Leaves are narrow-rounded at base, have many small sharp teeth. Flowers grow in sprays *around* the stems, and later develop the fruit in the same form—small dark red berries and quite puckery in taste.

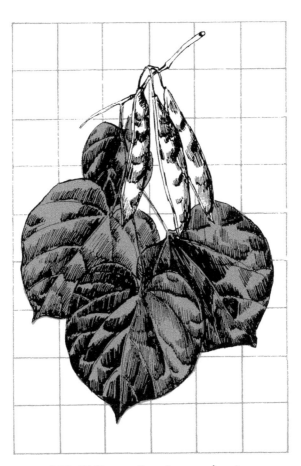

RED-BUD • Cercis canadensis

Shiny *heart-shaped* leaves, slightly hairy on underside. Grows on banks and slopes among larger trees, and blooms together with Dogwood. Flowers are lavender-pink and profuse in early spring. Bears a 3-inch fruit pod carrying oblong seeds. Small tree usually, rarely as tall as 30 feet. Other name: JUDAS TREE.

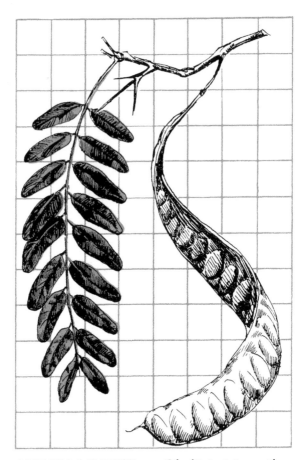

HONEY LOCUST • *Gleditsia triacanthos*

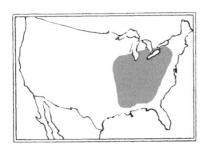

A big one, up to 125 foot height and 3 foot diameter. Bark is dark gray, scaly but not rough or ridged. Many thorns often three-pointed above each leaf joint. Leaves are 7 to 10 inches long, with twelve to eighteen leaflets of lance-shape, rather rounded at each end. Flowers grow in pale green clusters, and fruit pods (a foot or more long) are dark brown, twisted, and contain the *oval* seeds in a juicy pulp.

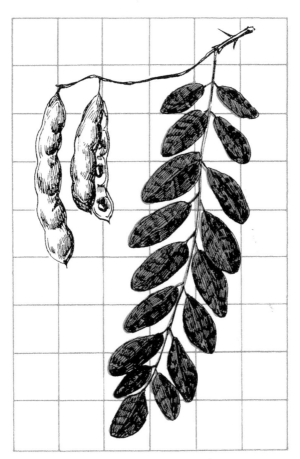

LOCUST • Robinia pseudoacacia

Bark of this one deeply ridged and rough. Grows to 75 feet, with twisty branches. Many *single-pointed* thorns. Leaves are compound (about 10 inches long usually) with leaflets of oval shape, rounded at both ends. Flowers sweet and yellowish-white. Fruit pods (2 to 4 inches long) are purplish and contain the *round* seeds.

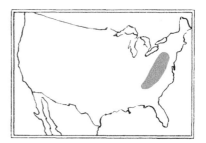

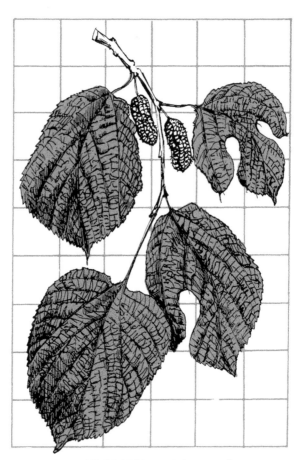

RED MULBERRY • Morus rubra

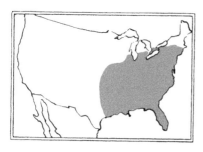

You will find mitten-shaped three-lobed, and roundish-oval leaves on Mulberry trees. All of them dark green above, toothed, and rough to touch. If the leafstalk is cut it exudes a milky fluid. Flowers are spiky, white, develop into the mulberry, a purplish fruit like an elongated blackberry, delicious in flavor. Average trees about 50 feet high, growing preferably in moist, rich soil. Other names: MULBERRY; BLACK MULBERRY.

PEAR THORN • Crataegus calpodendron

Hawthorn trees are so numerous that a whole book is needed to identify the species. The Pear Thorn is merely representative—all others are quite similar. The leaves are sharply toothed, the branches are contorted, and armed with long sharp thorns—these are common to all. So are the scarlet

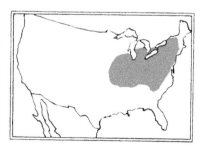

haws or berries that ripen in fall, often remain through the winter. None are tall—averaging up to 25 feet. Other names: HAWTHORN; HAW; THORN BUSH.

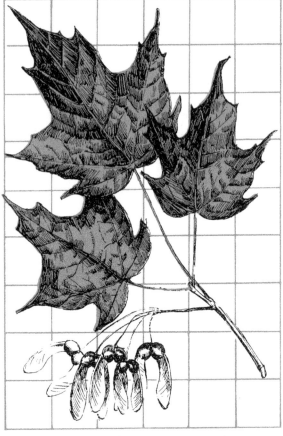

SUGAR MAPLE • Acer saccharum

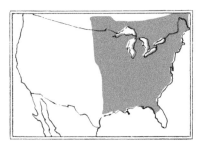

The leaves (opposite) have three to five points or lobes, with smooth edges, dark shining green above, paler, prominently veined beneath. Attains a height of 100 feet or so on well-drained uplands, tall in forests, rounded and symmetrical in open. Bark on mature trees is rough with pronounced vertical ridges, some protruding 3 to 4 inches. Other names: Rock Maple; Hard Maple. (Similar Black Maple usually has three-lobed leaves.)

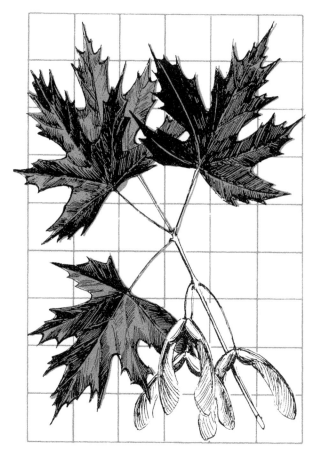

SILVER MAPLE • Acer saccharinum

Leaves have five lobes and are *deeply cut,* with varied but marked teeth, wedge-cut at stem; silvery white underneath, darker green above. Turns pale yellow in fall. Grows tall, over 100 feet, and does well in damp soil of bottom lands. The winged seeds are quite large— sometimes 2 inches spread. Other names: SILVER LEAF MAPLE; WHITE MAPLE; RIVER MAPLE.

RED MAPLE • Acer rubrum

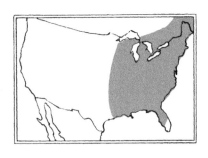

Notches between the three to five leaf-lobes are angular, not rounded, leaf stems are reddish. In early spring the crimson blossoms are profuse, and in fall whole tree is mass of bright red leaves. Something visibly red at all seasons of the year. Grows to 100 foot height, and is a lowland tree.

Other names: SCARLET MAPLE; SWAMP MAPLE; SOFT MAPLE.

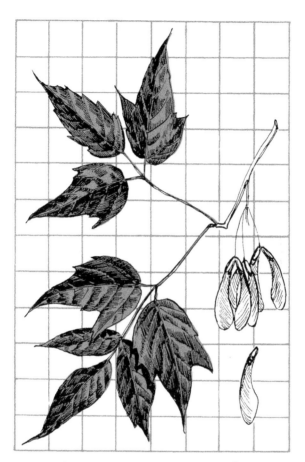

BOX ELDER • Acer negundo

Has compound leaves, with three to five leaflets. The end leaflets are lance-shaped, somewhat like Ash leaves, the two base leaflets wider and more of Maple form. A bottom land grower of 50 to 75 foot height. The winged seeds have a spread of 1½ to 2 inches. Other name: ASH-LEAVED MAPLE.

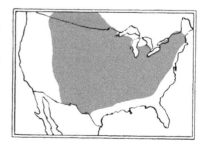

94

HORSE CHESTNUT • Aesculus hippocastanum

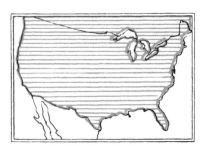

Leaves are compound, five to seven of them growing at the end of a stout stem. Flowers are waxy white, profuse, and spotted with purple and yellow, and grow in lilac-like clusters. The nut-husks are round, green and prickly, partitioned to hold two mahogany-brown large nuts. The leaf-scars on twigs look like tiny horseshoe marks. Other name: BUCKEYE.

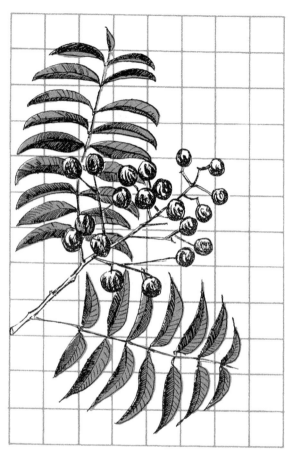

WESTERN SOAPBERRY • Sapindus drummondi

A southwestern tree, has compound leaves, with up to eleven pairs of sickle-shaped leaflets. The fruit grows in large deep-yellow clusters. The pulp of the berry is detergent and makes a lather when rubbed in water. Is a bottom land tree with rough scaly bark, roots spreading strongly at the base, and it grows to 75 foot height.

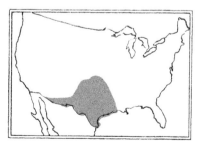

BASSWOOD • Tilia americana

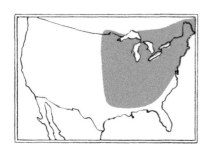

Big heart-shaped leaves, slightly lopsided. Buds are ruby colored. Blossoms are greenish-white, full of sweet nectar for bees, and develop into small nutlike fruits, each with one seed. Prefers rich well-drained soil and grows to great size—well over 100 feet—and is a splendid shade tree. Other name: LINDEN.

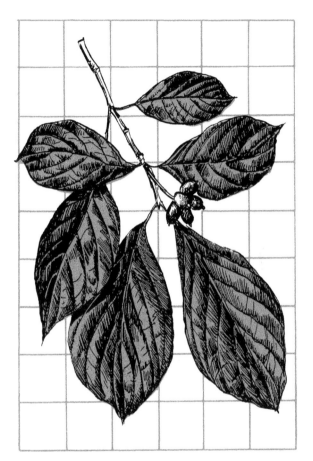

FLOWERING DOGWOOD • Cornus florida

Leaves are mostly *fat* ovals, rather thick, with veins on top depressed, on bottom in high relief; grow *opposite* on twig. Flower is yellowish-white, with four large petals. Bright scarlet berries, which are elongated ovals, form in late summer. Dogwood is most often seen as small tree—8 to 10 feet high

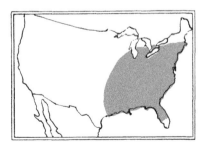

—growing well in drained soil in shade of larger trees.

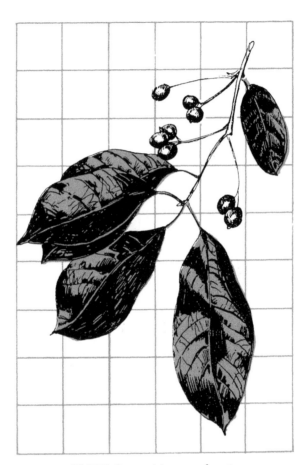

TUPELO • Nyssa sylvatica

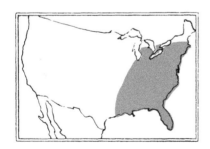

Shiny, thick, dark green leaves of oval shape—and 2 to 4 inches long. Fruit in fall is small cluster of two or three blue (almost black) berries, sour to taste. Tupelo grows to 100 feet in wet places, and has heavily ridged bark. Fall color — reddish-purple. Other names: SOUR GUM; PEPPERIDGE.

PERSIMMON • Diospyros virginiana

Dark brown bark broken into small blocks (like alligator hide). The oval leaves, 3 to 7 inches long, are dark green, shiny, and not toothed on margins. Fruit is a round berry about 1 inch in diameter, pale orange—very bitter and astringent when green, delicious when ripe. Sometimes reaches 100 foot height, usually 25 to 40. Other names: POSSUMWOOD; DATE PLUM.

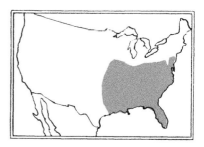

SNOWDROP TREE • Mohrodendron carolinum

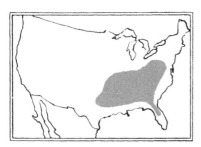

Leaves have depressed veins on top like the Dogwood, but are larger (4 to 6 inches long) and grow alternately on twig. Just a suggestion of teeth in margins. In spring bears many white bell-shaped flowers about ¾ of an inch long. It keeps company with Rhododendrons, Witch Hazel and such trees in rich well-drained soil. Usually a small tree or large shrub. Other name: SILVER BELL TREE.

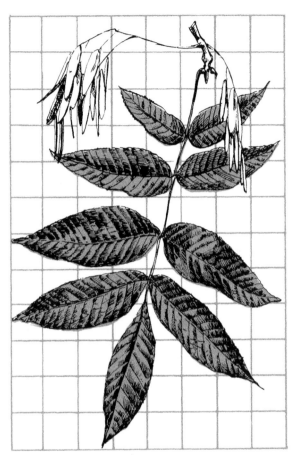

BLACK ASH • Fraxinus nigra

All the Ashes have *compound* leaves, with leaflets of same general oval shape. One quick clue to Ashes is the bark which is smooth above, rougher close to the ground. Somewhat like an elephant's leg. The Black Ash is instantly identified by the fact that the 7 to 11 leaflets *have no stems.* Seeds are

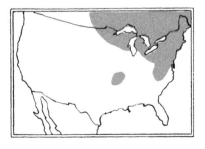

winged and grow in thick clusters. This tree is a 100-footer. Other names: HOOP ASH; BROWN ASH; BASKET ASH; SWAMP ASH.

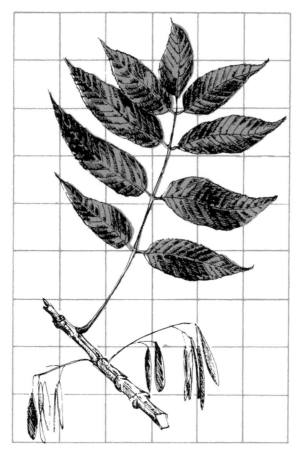

BLUE ASH • Fraxinus quadrangulata

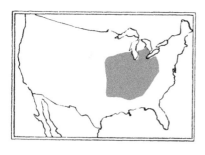

Leaves compound, opposite on twigs, and with seven to eleven leaflets on short, slightly hairy stems. The twigs are squarish in shape with four ridges running lengthwise — this is the certain identification. Another 100 foot tree, growing best in dry uplands. If in doubt, crush a little of the inner bark in water; it will show a bluish color. Outer bark on old trees is very ragged—like Shagbark Hickory.

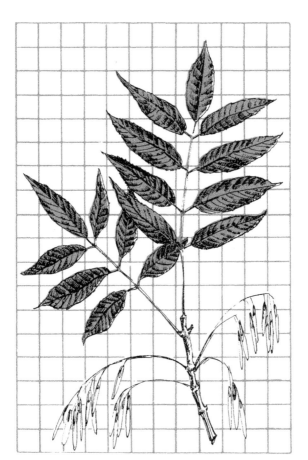

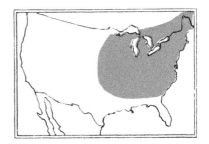

WHITE ASH • Fraxinus americana

Elongated *diamond-shaped* furrows on the lower trunk help identify White Ash. Leaflets (five to nine) on the compound leaves have stems of same length and are somewhat toothed on margins. The seed has a narrow wing and is 1 to 2 inches long. Grows tall—over 100 feet—in rich soil. Other name: AMERICAN ASH.

GREEN ASH • Fraxinus lanceolata

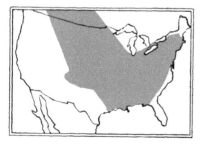

Leaves 8 to 12 inches long with five to nine lance-shaped leaflets are rather bright green on both sides. Sharply toothed and with very short stems. The winged seed is long, slender and shaped like a canoe paddle. Tree reaches 70 to 80 foot height on stream banks and lake shores, often in bottom lands. Bark similar to White Ash but diamond-shapes not so definite.

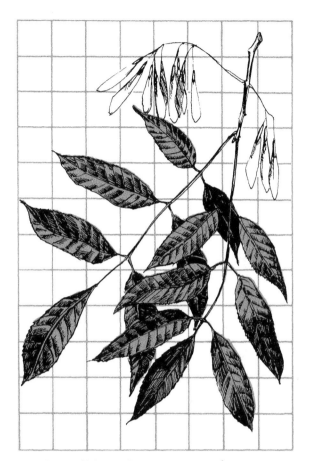

RED ASH • Fraxinus pennsylvanica

The seven to nine yellowish-green leaflets on the compound leaves are more widely spaced than other Ashes. Grows to about 50 foot height. You may need to cut to the inner bark of a branch and check the reddish color to be sure of identification.

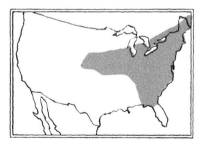

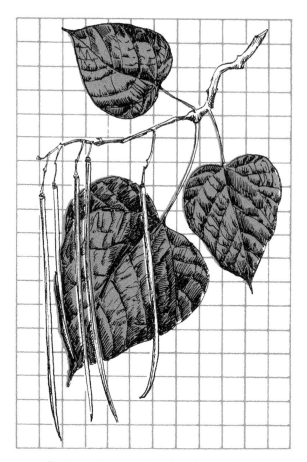

CATALPA • Catalpa bignonioides

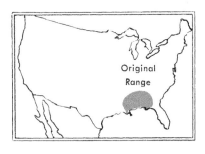

Original Range

106

Huge heart-shaped leaves, 6 to 12 inches long, and 4 to 5 inches wide. Early summer white flowers grow in drooping clusters (panicles) in great numbers. Later, winged seeds grow in long cigar-shaped pods. Grows sometimes to 50 feet, and now common east of Rockies. Other names: CIGAR TREE; INDIAN CIGAR TREE; EASTERN CATALAPA; BEAN TREE; INDIAN BEAN.

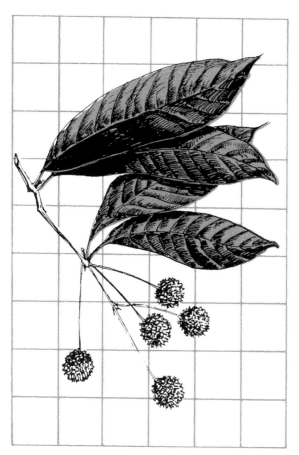

BUTTON-BUSH • Cephalanthus occidentalis

Widely distributed coast to coast, usually a shrub, but in southwest reaching 40 to 50 feet. Found by "slow water" in swamps or ponds. Gets name from ½-inch round "button" fruit in heads growing on the ends of twigs. Oval leaves, dark green above, and with smooth margins are 4 to 7 inches long. Between stems are small leaflike triangular parts. Other name: BOTTOM-BUSH.

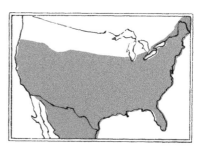

CHESTNUT • Castanea dentata

108

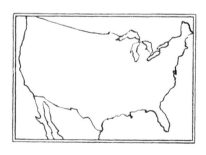

A blight has all but wiped out this favorite American tree, but we include it for sentimental reasons and in hope of its revival. The six to nine lance-shaped leaves have pronounced sharply pointed teeth. Fruit—several delicious brown nuts in protective prickly bur. A big one, often more than 100 feet high, with deeply furrowed gray-brown bark. A tree of fond memory.

TREES IN WINTER

It takes devoted years of study to make positive identification of trees in winter. Most people do not even try. But Rutherford Platt developed a copyrighted chart to help give some clues to trees when the leaves are off, and has kindly granted permission to include this information here. He says: "It's fun to be a tree detective in winter. When trees are bare of leaves they still have many clues to answer the question: 'what kind of tree is that?' All you need is a twig or two." The text appeared in Mr. Platt's fine book *This Green World*.

ABOUT RUTHERFORD PLATT

A man with huge curiosity . . . plus cameras, plus a lively interest in nature, plus a brilliant ability to impart his nature lore in charming style. His book *This Green World,* published by Dodd, Mead & Co., won for Mr. Platt the John Burroughs Medal in 1945 for the year's "foremost literary work in a field so eminently occupied by the great American naturalist." His *Our Flowering World* and *American Trees* are books of great value and real importance in the nature field.

BUDS
Opposite

DIRECTIONS

FIRST look for the buds. Note their arrangement, shape, size, and scales. Pay special attention to buds at end of twig.

SECOND look for the leaf scar. Note its shape and the dots in it.

THIRD look for other clues. These may or may not be present; bright colors, thorns, catkins, peculiarities of pith, twig, or bark.

Answer questions that follow as though "true or false." If the first A does not fit, go on to the next A. When A fits, then take B under the A that fits. So on, until you reach the answer.

EXPLANATION
OF CERTAIN WORDS

LEAF SCAR: Mark on twig where last season's leaf fell from stem. Usually found just below bud.

BUD SCALES: The hard outer covering of buds.

PITH PARTITIONS: The pith is the core of a twig. When sliced lengthwise you sometimes see partitions like the rounds of a ladder.

CATKINS: These are little stiff tassels (often 1 or 2 inches long) that hang on some trees. Usually found on the birches.

WITCHES' BROOMS: Seen on the hackberry, like a dark bunch or tangle of twigs.

BUDS
Alternate

(A) BUDS OPPOSITE

(B) BUDS LARGE (½ to 1 inch or longer) blunt, oval . . . . HORSE CHESTNUT

(B) BUDS SMALL (½ inch or less)

(C) SCALES MEETING AT EDGES. Bud on end of twig like a silver-gray shoe-button with four scales . . . . FLOWERING DOGWOOD

(C) SCALES OVERLAPPING

(D) Buds oval, those at end of twig in threes with middle one much longer. Leaf scars narrow, triangular with three dots . . . . MAPLE

(D) Buds fatter, dark brown. Buds at end of twig close together making fancy design. Leaf scars shield shape, or almost circular, with many dots forming a horseshoe . . . . . . ASH

Overlapping Scales

Single Scale covering Bud

(A) BUDS IN WHORLS OF THREE

Tiny fat buds. Leaf scars round, standing out on platforms; two large scars and one small scar in each whorl . . . . CATALPA

(A) BUDS ALTERNATE

(B) SAP MILKY

1. Buds triangular with two or three red-brown scales . . . . MULBERRY

2. Tiny brown buds and powerful thorns . . .
OSAGE ORANGE

3. Pith orange, small tree or shrub . . SUMAC

Two Scales like a valve

Naked (No Scales)

(B) SAP NOT MILKY
(C) WITH THORNS
1. Buds sunken out of sight in bark, thorns slender, *branched*................HONEY LOCUST
2. Buds sunken out of sight in bark, thorns thick, unbranched, *in pairs* at leaf scars.............
BLACK LOCUST
3. Single thorns, from side of twig; buds minute
HAWTHORN
4. Single heavy thorn from end of short branch
PEAR
(C) WITHOUT THORNS
(D) PITH WITH PARTITIONS
1. Spaces between partitions empty. No scales on buds ....WALNUT
2. Pith white, buds light brown with two scales like a duck's bill.............TULIP TREE
3. Pith partitions unequally spaced. Buds dark red-brown with about four scales........TUPELO
4. Pith partitions unequally spaced. Buds dark, triangular. Bark in square chunks   PERSIMMON
5. Partitions close together. Bark warty. "Witches' brooms" often visible.........HACKBERRY
(D) PITH WITHOUT PARTITIONS
(E) WITH CATKINS
1. Bark smooth, or papery and curly....BIRCH
2. Bark in narrow, ragged vertical strips.......
HOP HORNBEAM
(E) WITHOUT CATKINS
(F) BUDS USUALLY CLUSTERED TOWARD TIP OF TWIG............................OAK
(F) BUDS NOT USUALLY CLUSTERED TOWARD TIP OF TWIG
(G) WITH DISTINCTIVE TWIGS
1. Twigs green with spicy taste....SASSAFRAS
2. Older twigs with corky ridges and wings. Buds mahogany-brown, shiny.........SWEET GUM
3. Young twigs red above, green beneath......
PEACH
4. Twigs with bitter taste like cherry pits. (Young bark smooth like birch).............CHERRY

(G) WITHOUT DISTINCTIVE TWIGS

(H) NO SCALES ON BUDS. Tiny folded leaves of buds sulphur yellow...BITTERNUT HICKORY

(H) ONE SCALE SHOWING ON BUDS

1. End bud big, sometimes an inch long, oval, hairy . . . . MAGNOLIA

2. Buds like light brown conical hats. Leaf scar makes narrow circle around base of bud. . . . .
SYCAMORE

3. Buds red, pressed against twig. . . . . WILLOW

(H) TWO SCALES SHOWING ON BUD

1. Little round buds set into the top of a big oval leaf scar. About nine dots just inside edge of leaf scar . . . . AILANTHUS

2. Green or red scales,. one of which bulges, making bud lopsided. . . . . LINDEN

3. End bud fat, wide oval. Scales soft, light gray, or tan. (Note: the tough outside scales fall off early). . . . . MOCKERNUT HICKORY
or PIGNUT HICKORY

(H) THREE SCALES SHOWING ON BUD

Buds smooth, oval, brown. Pith star shaped in cross-section . . . . CHESTNUT

(H) MORE THAN THREE SCALES SHOWING ON BUD

1. Inner scales soft gray. Outer scales with long points. . . . . SHAGBARK HICKORY

2. Light brown. Longest, sharpest of all buds. (Often ¾ inch long). . . . . BEECH

3. About six scales arranged in two vertical rows. Bud usually tipped and on one side of leaf scar
ELM

4. Long sharp buds often shiny as though varnished and pressed close to twig. Pith star shaped in cross-section. POPLAR

5. Blunt, wooly, so that scales may not show clearly. Squatty tree. Trunk often leaning. . APPLE

BARE TREES OF THE WINTER LANDSCAPE

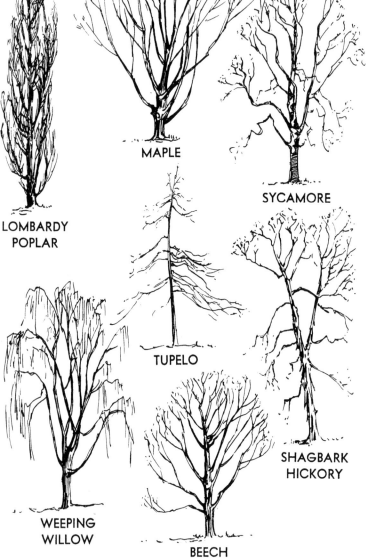

LOMBARDY
POPLAR

MAPLE

SYCAMORE

TUPELO

WEEPING
WILLOW

BEECH

SHAGBARK
HICKORY

. . . TYPICAL SHAPES

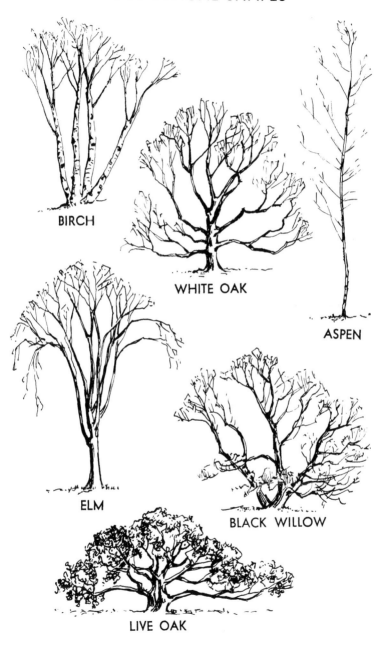

BIRCH

WHITE OAK

ASPEN

ELM

BLACK WILLOW

LIVE OAK

DETECTING THE EVERGREENS

People often confuse evergreen names, although they can be easily identified.

The trees commonly known as evergreens are members of the Pine Family. Their leaves are needles, and they produce cones. A few trees in other families with broad leaves are also evergreen. This is true of the Live Oak, Magnolia, and Rhododendron. On the other hand, two members of the Pine Family are not evergreens: the Larch and the Bald Cypress shed their needles in winter.

The native American evergreens that you commonly see decorating the winter landscape with their dark green foliage are easy to recognize if you look closely at the twigs. Here is a pictorial key that tells you what to look for.

If you know these six kinds, you will be an evergreen detective. You will enjoy an acquaintance with all the evergreens you see except cultivated kinds and some that are restricted in their distribution.

PINE

Long needles held together at the base by a sheath of papery bark. The number of needles in each cluster tells you the kind of Pine. For example: White Pine, five needles; Red Pine, two needles; Pitch Pine, three needles.

FIR

The only native Fir east of the Rockies is the Balsam. Needles in two ranks make a flat design. Pluck off needle and you see on the twig a little round scar with a dot in the center.

HEMLOCK

Needles in two ranks like the Fir, but shorter, flatter, and blunt. Dark green and shiny above, pale below with two parallel dotted lines. Along top of twig you see little upside-down needles.

JUNIPER

Common tree form called Red Cedar whose red heartwood scares off moths. Two kinds of needles often grow on same shoot: sharp awl-shaped projecting at angles, and flat overlapping scales that hug the twig.

SPRUCE

Needles are short, four-sided (awl-shaped), arranged in spirals on the twig. Pluck off needles and you see their stems left on the twig like little hooks or projections.

WHITE CEDAR

Common form called Arborvitae. Needles in four ranks, flat, shiny and overlapping closely, forming geometric design. Center needles with dots. (Drawings are greatly magnified.)

SOME TYPICAL EVERGREEN SHAPES IN WINTER

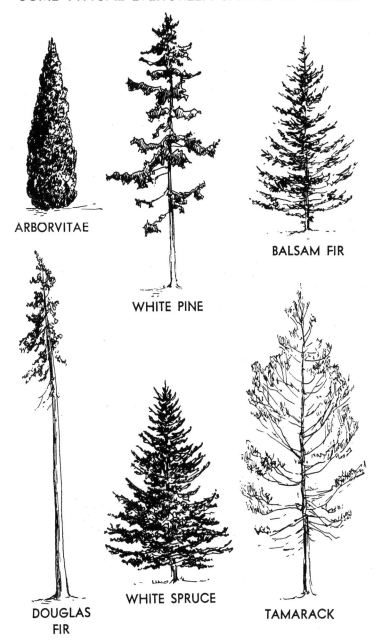

ARBORVITAE

WHITE PINE

BALSAM FIR

DOUGLAS FIR

WHITE SPRUCE

TAMARACK

MORE EVERGREEN SILHOUETTES IN WINTER

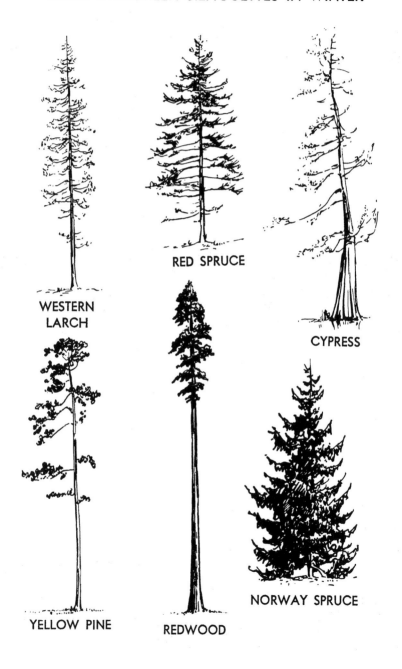

WESTERN
LARCH

RED SPRUCE

CYPRESS

YELLOW PINE

REDWOOD

NORWAY SPRUCE

INDEX

125